the wild part

Carolyn Duncan

Presentation by *BookLeaf Publishing*

Web: www.bookleafpub.com

E-mail: info@bookleafpub.com

ISBN: 9789395784207

First edition 2023

DEDICATION

To Angie and Blue.

the wild part

There are certain deaths
for which there are no funerals.
I thought the wild part in me
called to the wild part in you.
But now there is only silence.

So I have set my love away,
deep in the darkest woods
that have been forgotten even by song.

I have set away longing.
I have set away the dream of you.

I have set away the darkness
and terror of abandonment.
I have set away trying to understand why you
made me hold your pain.
And as the fog falls away, finally,
I am free.

Country

I dream of a country undiscovered by all maps,
where I can rewrite myself
in the freedom of a decolonized body.
Where I can close my grief like a door
on the pain of history.

But I am only here,
where the winter numbs me to my core.
The city is stagnant and damp.
It smells of rotting leaves and garbage.
Memory will not let us go.

what the visible world conceals

I sit at the edge of evening,
watching the rivers of lights
as cars move along the streets.
Lights go on and off
in windows across the way.

I watch the night lengthen
Like a shadow across the world.
It smells like rain, leaves, hours passing,
like the world that the visible world conceals,
language seeking to articulate the self
like the blind mouths of baby birds.

Somewhere music plays and someone laughs.
The sounds go by too.
Memory is like a refrain
just fading from the ear.

Sepulveda Afternoon

In the fading afternoon light
the blue shadows mingled and stretched away in
the dim light and sounds
of a Sunday afternoon.

The streets were nearly empty,
the sentiment nearly gone,
the sunlight too hesitant to dull despair
but too bright to offer the relief of night.

Hopper

He painted around the emptiness,
rather than over it, or away from it.
Sometimes it was a crowded city street,
sometimes an empty landscape at night.

In my dream he said,
This is how God made the universe.
This is why it is defined and yet infinite --
because it is wrapped around emptiness.

Adjustments

She makes some adjustments, required revisions
to accommodate the abandonment. Maybe
she takes things too seriously. Maybe
she loves too hard. Maybe
she needs too much. Maybe
she is better off alone.

Eventually, she realizes that the problem
is not hers to own.
Some people are not ready to be loved.
Sometimes the greatest hurt that can be done
is simply not caring enough.

Hope

Is a little house with a yard.
Summer light in the grass
as the dogs scout for worms to roll in,
a breeze that lifts leaves on trees
like hair off a woman's neck.
There is a room for reading and writing,
and the forest spans the hills.

At night the trains fly through the hills
like birds skimming the sea's surface.
The kitchen fills with warm light
and the sounds of the dogs rattling their bowls.
The stars fold themselves into the dark sky,
ready for sleep.

Walking Near Death Valley

I walked around the desolate crater
like an astronaut in an alien landscape.
Sometimes the wind sang a dirge
among the insurmountable mountains,
and the dry grasses that waved like ghosts.

I walked as if the ritual could lift the weight
I carried everywhere.
Grief has perched in my body
and made its home,
holding a broken bone
where my breath should be.

I can only take solace in the wild earth,
the seasons:
even when it seems like this will never end,
there is an end to everything.

reckoning

the faded clouds trail across the bright sky,
as the red and yellow cactus flowers
announce themselves among the dead rocks.

i am surprised to find
i resent the persistent desert,
that is here when he is not.
that i am here when he is not.
fitting that the word desert
also means to leave, abandon.

the desert tries to surprise me
with purple flowers --
there is color here
even among the dust and jagged rocks,
the shadows that stretch
and mark a further distance.
there is life even here. and yet he is not.
it hurts to even breathe.

i climb the stones to the summit, and
weave grief into the night.
cast a spell to bring me home,
to meaning erased by loss,
lost, among the dry plains,
the knotted trees and sleepy lizards,
the texture of grief.

Loss During the Pandemic

"I never knew that grief felt so much like fear."
My dog and I take long walks in the park.
Walks to forget, for a little while,
about all the loss.

Grief is now something I carry around, always.
It never disappears. It only changes shape.
Grief means I loved you.
Grief means I carry you with me.
Grief means that I am still here,
somehow, holding your memory.

Angie

My dog curls on herself like a comma,
her left ear folded like a bookmark.
Her paws smell like corn muffins,
and her body like the sun.
When she plays outside, she brings back
the smell of freshly cut grass.
She has no existential questions, except:
next treat? Ball? Park? Walk?
These good little things.
Happiness --
with a lick and a tail flick --
is standing right there.

Vaquera

The stars pinned themselves
to the dark fabric of the night
as she rested on the dusty banks.
She was one of the last vaqueras.
She knew the scent of the sun-warmed earth,
the sound of leaves in the rain,
and the texture of untraveled roads.
She wasn't afraid of solitude, or scorpions,
or not knowing the exact time.

That didn't mean that loneliness didn't cut
like lightning painting a hot sky.
But she knew the difference between
settling and wishing
in the night's blue dark.

Receipt

"Paper curled sideways,
the smell of pine and fallen leaves.
Loss unexchangeable."
I find these words years later
and do not recall their origin.

I do know that faith is not a deity for me.
It is not a given, nor stable.
It is like the tide, ebbing and flowing.
Sometimes it feels easier to drown.
In such moments, I find the summer sun and my
dog's contented sigh
sufficient exchange for one more day of hope.

the world swims to consciousness

outside the rain pummels down
rushing towards gutters
(carrying leaves)
as the sounds lap against memory.
she brushes the hair back from her eyes.
the city lights look like smears of color painted
with a brush
through her rain-blurred windows.
the strange landscape of untraveled time
stretches out before her,
mapped against the visible world.

Preservation in Amber

The cool afternoon fades
as gray spreads out against the sky.
The bees sing out of tune
with the hum of power lines.
Moths circle the streetlights
as if in afterthought.

I am here despite memory,
though recollection suggests
that these bones and skin become unhinged,
and dance to a melancholy song
of a childhood of constant storms.

The moths flutter against the screen door.
Streetlights illuminate their persistence,
wings fluttering darkly:
a grief that must be let in.

Ghost

All we are is distance.
My memory of you
is a crack in the windowpane
that lets a cold ghost
into the warm room.

Now I can only love backwards, through
memory.
Just as I love the rainy city,
plastered with red and yellow leaves,
the turrets of ambitious houses
and ineloquent advertisements
in all their fumbled grace.

The moon rises over the billboards,
couples under umbrellas,
Buses filled with blue light
and tired faces at the windows.
Love is possibly impossible in this world.
Yet love still stains me
like ink upon my hand,
like the smoke of wildfires in the air.

The city settles into the night.
Sometimes loss looks like hesitation.

Pluck love, and bite
until the cold seeps through
like a jolt to the head —

Absence

The leaves turn into a red of longing,
chance, regret.
In the nights, trains howl like human voices
and fade into the dark hills of the republic.
The sky turns from pale to black
like a page stained with ink.
I wonder where words go
when pain refuses a reason or an exit.

And in the night sky above me,
the Milky Way spills chalk dust across the sky,
as if someone tried to write a formula
to explain it all,
and wound up writing an old lullaby.

Blue's Poem

The sky filled with puffy clouds
and the fields became the Sargasso Sea
as the wind created waves of grass.
I could forget the troublesome neighbor,
the break-up, but not death that had chased me
for two years,
trying to take chunks of me away.

Grief is the heavy stone we push up a hill,
the work of love and memory.
How I loved my dogs, their corn-scented paws,
the soft down of their fur,
how they smelled like grass
and wind after being outdoors.
In my love for them, I found
a tenderness and innocence
that I thought I was too afraid to ever know.

Seeds

In the wild country of your heart,
in the plains of your body,
did you feel the sky stretch to the horizon,
promising infinity?

You clawed your fingers in the dirt
and set the seeds of hope like little teeth:
sharp and absolute.